THE ADVENTURES OF BENMORE DOGS

By
Lauren Meehan

Copyright

Copyright © 2023 Laureen Meehan

All rights reserved. No part of this book may be reproduced without prior written permission from the Author.

Dedication

For my amazing family and partner. I can't thank them enough for the amazing support that I have received from them. Truly, without them, I wouldn't be able to achieve my goals in life, and this book is one of my greatest achievements.

Acknowledgment

I would like to extend my heartfelt gratitude toward my family and my partner because they never gave up on me and never stopped believing. Without them, I would have never been able to author something as impeccable as this. Truth be told, I want this book to be cherished and I want it to serve as an instrument of inspiration for readers all around the world.

CONTENTS

CHAPTER 1: THE THREE FURRY SIBLINGS — 13

CHAPTER 2: LET'S SAVE THE FOREST! — 20

CHAPTER 3: TOGETHER WE CAN MAKE A DIFFERENCE — 26

CHAPTER 4: A FRIEND IN NEED IS A FRIEND INDEED — 32

CHAPTER 5: THE MAJESTIC UNICORN — 40

CHAPTER 6: ANIMALS IN DISTRESS — 47

CHAPTER 7: THE POOR LAMB — 57

CHAPTER 8: OVERCOMING ONE HURDLE AFTER ANOTHER — 61

CHAPTER 9: BEST FRIENDS FOREVER — 67

CHAPTER 1:
THE THREE FURRY SIBLINGS

Once upon a time, three furry siblings lived in a lovely house in the suburbs: Joey, Sky, and Woody. Joey was a brown dog with floppy ears, Woody was a black and white dog with pointy ears, and Sky was a fluffy white dog with big brown eyes, and she was the only girl in their gang.

It was a beautiful day in the backyard, and Woody, Sky, and Joey were eager to play. The sun was shining brightly, casting a warm glow over the grass. A gentle breeze carried the scent of fresh flowers, filling the air with a sweet fragrance. With his fluffy coat, Woody ran towards Sky and Joey, his tail wagging enthusiastically.

"Hey guys, what's up?" he barked.

Sky was very sleek; she playfully nipped at Woody's ear. "Just enjoying this gorgeous day, Woody. Let's play some fetch!" she said.

Joey, a lovable dog with a playful personality, wagged his tail in agreement. "Yeah, let's fetch some balls!" he barked excitedly.

The trio raced across the yard, chasing the bright orange ball Woody had retrieved from the toy chest. They barked and growled playfully, jumping and twisting in the air as they tried to catch the ball in mid-flight. The sun shone down as they played, warming their fur and making them feel alive. The birds sang merrily in the trees, adding to the cheerful atmosphere.

Suddenly the ball got stuck in between one of the branches of the big old tree in their backyard. The three dogs stood under it, staring at their ball in confusion about how to get it out.

"Sky, you're the fastest and lightest. Can you try to get up there?" asked Woody.

Sky looked at him with a strange face and called him silly,

"How do you expect me to get up there? I'm not a cat. Maybe we can get Tinker to help us. She could climb that tree in no time. Should I go get her?" explained sky as she excitedly wagged her tail.

"Guys, come on, we are three smart dogs. I think we can get a silly old ball out of the tree on our own," said Joey.

Sky and Woody both looked at him, expecting an answer on how to do that. The three siblings then tried so many things to get the ball. They tried to poke it with a long stick. Joey and Woody both grabbed a stick firmly with their mouths and tried to push the ball out of the tree, but it didn't work. Sky then had another idea, and she tossed a frisbee up toward the ball. It hit the ball once, but not hard enough. On the last throw, Sky tossed the frisbee so hard it flew into the neighbor's yard.

Lost and confused, the three siblings give up when Joey suddenly has an idea. "Sky, you're the lightest, so you will have to do this. I will stand under the tree, Woody will get on top of me, and you will get on top of Woody. That way, we can get higher, and you can poke the ball out with our stick." Said, Joey.

Everyone got excited and started wagging their tails. They quickly gathered everything they needed to perform the task. Joey pulled out one of their toy boxes to get some extra height. He jumped on it and asked Woody to climb on top of him.

"Careful now, don't fall." Said Joey calmly.

"I know, I know. Shh, you're making me nervous." Replied Woody as he slowly climbed on top of Joey.

And so, Sky followed their lead. "Hey! Stop moving." She screamed as she was climbing on top.

Joey and Woody giggled under her. Everyone was set and ready to do their jobs. Sky pulled the stick up with her mouth and began poking it. It was a little hard because the ball was really jammed in there, but after a few pushes, she managed to do it, and their ball fell to the ground.

The three siblings all jumped down and began racing each other in excitement. They laughed and celebrated until they were out of breath.

"That was amazing. Look how we managed to do something like that with teamwork, all we need is each other, and we can do anything," said Joey with a big smile on his face.

They loved to play together in their big backyard, chasing each other around and barking at the birds in the trees. One day, they decided to play tag when Woody slipped on a patch of wet grass and fell on his backside. Sky and Joey started laughing at him, and Woody couldn't help but join in too.

"You guys are hilarious," Woody said between laughs.

"We always have so much fun together," Sky added.

"But sometimes I feel like we're doing the same things every day," Joey said. "I'm getting a little bored of it."

Woody and Sky agreed with Joey.

"We need to do something new and exciting," Sky said.

"But what?" Woody asked.

They all thought for a moment until they heard a car engine start-up. They looked over and saw their neighbor, Tinker the cat, and her family getting into their car. "Where do you think they're going?" Joey wondered aloud.

As Tinker's car pulled out of the driveway and drove down the street, Joey, Sky, and Woody all felt a pang of jealousy. They wished they were going on a trip too. Tinker, along with her family, was going on what appeared to be a vacation. They had so many bags packed that they were loaded onto their truck one by one. They were annoyed from playing the same thing all day that they immediately decided to come up with a fun plan of their own, but as Joey was giving them ideas, the sky let out a big yawn.

"Can I take a small nap before we do that? I'm really tired." She replied. Woody agreed with Sky as he yawned as well. They all decided to take a nap. They all raced to their beds and hopped on. As the three siblings snuggled up next to each other, they told each other that they would talk in a few hours.

Joey woke up. First, he stretched his little paws as he pushed both Sky and Woody out of bed. They woke up annoyed and shook their tails. Now awake a refreshed, the gang was ready to make a plan.

"Okay, guys," Joey said. "We need to figure out something new to do." Sky and Woody nodded in agreement.

"What if we go on an adventure?" Woody suggested.

"Like where?" Sky asked.

"I don't know," Woody said. "But we could explore the neighborhood and see what we find."

Joey liked the idea of going on an adventure.

"But we need to be careful," he said. "We don't want to get lost or get into any trouble."

Sky agreed. "We should stay close to home," she said. "But there are still lots of things to see and discover." With their plan in place, the three dogs set out into the neighborhood. They trotted down the sidewalk, sniffing at everything they passed. They saw other dogs barking in their yards, squirrels running up trees, and birds flying overhead. They even found a park with a pond and ducks swimming in it.

As they were walking, Joey sighed and said, "when I said we need to find something else to do, this is not what I had in mind, guys."

Sky and Woody both stopped in their tracks to turn around and look at him. They were confused. "I meant we should maybe...I don't know. Doing something meaningful. Bring happiness to someone, help someone in need."

Joey suggested they turn back home because they still needed time to make a plan, and mum would be worried. So, they all turned around and headed home, the sun was setting, and the sky was now a shade of yellow. Everything on the way back had a shadow, even the dogs. Sky found that very funny.

Just as they were entering their house, their mum called them in for food. They ran into the kitchen and gobbled up their dinner. Sky was the slowest eater because she was the smallest. Joey was the fastest. He would eat all of his food in a few minutes and make a mess while doing it. Woody, however, was always picky. He always threw a tantrum before eating his food, but after a few words from mum, he would buckle up and just finish his meal.

CHAPTER 2:
LET'S SAVE THE FOREST!

The next day the three fluff balls, Joey, Sky, and Woody, were all sleeping in their beds peacefully. Joey's paw was in Woody's face. Woody's Tail was in Joey's eyes. They both slept like that, always snuggled up next to each other. However, Sky preferred her own space. She wouldn't mind sleeping next to her brothers for a short Nap, but buckling down for the night, she needed to be in her own area for that.

It was early in the morning, but they were all still fast asleep, without a care in the world. Mum had called on them, but they didn't hear her. The light from their dolphin-printed curtains seeped in with a faint shimmer of yellow. The room was quiet, the only sound being the soft huffs and puffs from the three dogs. Sky was the first one to wake up. She slowly opened her eyes and stretched her legs. And then slowly got up and glanced over at her brothers. After getting out of bed, she did a little shake and yawned.

"Hey, guys, wake up! Hello?" she whispered, not trying to be loud. The boys didn't budge at all, so she just left to greet mum. She went down to the kitchen, and Mum was there waiting for her.

"Come here, my little darling." Said mum in the softest voice as she bent down to pet Sky. Sky licked her on the hands as Mum gave her a good rub on the belly.

"Sky sweetie, can you go wake your brother up? It's time for your breakfast." She said. Sky ran up to their room again and barked as loud as she could. Both Joey and Woody fell out of bed in a frenzy.

"Hey, why are you being so loud...". Growled Woody as he scratched his ear. Joey was still making sense of things and suddenly jumped in the air with excitement.

"I almost forgot, we have to plan out our adventure today." He said as he ran out of the room, Sky and Joey looked at each other with a funny looks and ran behind him. Downstairs they were all met with their breakfast bowls. In haste, they all ate everything as fast as they could so they could get started on their plan.

The three dogs then race each other outside to the yard, where they quickly jump into the sandbox and start messing around. They were giggling and laughing as the cloudy blue sky hung over them, throwing sand at each other.

"Okay, okay, enough messing around. Let's decide now. Everybody needs to come up with one idea about what we should do and think long and hard before answering because it's very important we get this right." Explained Joey.

"Oh, I know, you guys are going to love this. Last night I had a perfect dream about the beach. Why don't we take a trip there, it will be so much fun. Said Sky with a wagging tail. Joey and Woody liked the idea. But the sky wasn't done with her argument. She then started drawing in the sand with her little paws. She drew a boat, water, a beach ball, and an umbrella.

"Okay, now I need you both to lay down next to me and close your eyes, picture the image I am about to create with my words." Said sky with a smile on her face. As they all lay down in the sand and closed their eyes, Sky began telling her story.

"The windy sea breeze in your ears as it brushes your fur. The sweet smell of the ocean lingered in the air. There is sand as far as your eye can look where you can run as fast as you can without ever needing to stop, you can dig as many holes as you want, and the best part is. Mum wouldn't even get mad. We could play with our ball all day in the sun without the worry of tossing it into the neighbor's garden. Mum can even buy us all popsicles if we're lucky. We can do anything at the beach, go into the sea and get our paws wet. I can't swim, so you guys can even go do that. Anything you can think of, we can do it." Describe Sky in the most detailed way.

The boys loved her idea, but there were still two more candidates that needed to share their ideas before anybody decided on anything. Joey asked Woody to go next as he wanted to save his idea for last.

Woody excitedly then gets up and starts shoving the sand here and there, messing up Sky's drawing.

"Hey, watch it!" she screamed.

"I'm sorry, Sky, but you had your turn; now it's mine, and my plan is going to be ten times more fun," he said as he moved his paw around in the sand.

Both Sky and Joey looked at him and his drawing with concentration and wondered what he was making. Woody was not a good artist, but he tried.

"Tada! I'm going to be taking you all to the... drum roll please, AMUSEMENT PARK!" He screamed in excitement.

Everyone giggled as they all laid back down on the sand and closed their little eyes, ready for Woody's story.

"Okay, picture this. Mum and dad drive us up the city to the amusement park, we can do so many things there. We can all get on the Ferris wheel, I've seen pictures of it, and it looks so much fun. We can stick our heads out of the window and feel the wind on our tongues when we are high up in the sky.

Sky cut him off as he was speaking, "Wait, I can't get on that. No way I'm too scared of heights," she said.

"Oh, Sky, please don't interrupt me. You had your chance. Besides, there's nothing to be scared of, silly. Joey and I will hold your paw. Okay, where was I? Yes, after the Ferris wheel, we can try the roller coaster. It goes so fast that you guys will love it. Imagine sticking your head out of the car but ten times better. And the bumper cars, the boats, there's so much to do. I'm getting excited just thinking about it. And after that, we can even get hot dogs, a hot juicy bun stuffed with beef sausage, topped with ketchup and mustard. Wouldn't that be nice? If mum and dad let us stay a little longer, we can watch the amusement park lights at night. I have heard they are beautiful. Well, what do you guys think?" He asked as he got up with his tail already wagging, eagerly waiting for Joey and Sky to answer.

"That sounds like a fun plan." Said Sky, "what do you think, Joey?"

"Oh yeah, we can do that. It sounds like a lot of fun, too. Let's take a poll in the end, shall we, because I'm still left, and I think we all still need to think bigger." He said. As Joey begins preparing to tell everyone about his plan, they all overhear the news from inside, it catches their attention, and they all go inside, running and stop right in front of the TV and sit down and stare at the screen.

"The animals have all been displaced as the wildfire slowly takes over the entire forest, the rivers have dried up, making it difficult for water-based animals to survive, and some areas have been flooded with dangerous, dirty water from acid rain. It has been complete and utter chaos as we report to you live. Trees have fallen, disrupting birds. As you can see here, we have a poor Lion wandering, all muddy and sad. He appears to have lost his home because it is strange for this animal to be seen in this part of the land. What fears us most is that no attempts are being made to save wildlife or the forest. It has been like this for days, and I fear if this keeps up, we may see a lot more wildlife in trouble. This is Ashley King from Channel Six news, reporting live. I'll see you after the break." Says the reporter on the TV.

Mum switches off the TV, and the dogs just sit there in silence. They all look at each other with their mouth open, absolutely heartbroken to see all the animals losing their homes and loved ones like that.

"Okay, change of plans. I know what we're doing. We're going to save the forest!" said Joey with a big smile on his face.

Sky and Woody got so excited they started jumping up and down. Everyone instantly agreed on the plan and got to work.

Chapter 3:
Together We Can Make a Difference

"Are you sure we're not forgetting anything?" asked Sky as she stood on the driveway of her house, waiting for Joey and Woody to come out. It was a bright sunny day, perfect for an adventure. A cool breeze made it seem like it was summertime, but it was spring. The smell of freshly cut grass lingered from the lawn that dad had just mowed. It was all very beautiful, and Sky couldn't wait for her brothers to come out so they could get going.

"Hello? Are you guys coming, or do I leave without you?" asked Sky in a loud voice as Joey and Woody came running outside, fighting over a hat that both wanted to wear.

"It's my turn to wear it, Woody. You wore it last time at the park, remember?" Said Joey as he tried to tug it away from Woody.

"No, that was you, silly. It's my turn." Replied Woody.

"Sky watched both of them with an annoyed face, so she had an idea. While the two of them were fighting over the hat, she quietly snuck up behind them, snatched it off Woody's head, and wore it herself.

"Hey!" said Woody, "Give that back."

"Ha-ha, nice one, Sky. If I can't wear it, you can't either." Replied Joey with a smirk on his face.

Sky giggled as she spun around with the hat, "it looks much better on me anyway. Also, can we get going now? You two have already wasted so much time." She explained.

So, the three fluffballs set on their way to save the forest, the journey was long, but they had planned it all out. They began walking down the sidewalk, and after an hour of walking, they all felt exhausted. Joey pointed at an old oak tree.

"Look, guys, why don't we rest for a little bit? We have been walking for a while now, and I'm a little tired." He said.

Both Sky and Woody nodded in agreement, and so the three siblings settled down on a soft patch of grass under the tree. Suddenly everything felt peaceful, the excitement of reaching their destination was still there, but the peace and quiet of sitting in the cool shade of an oak tree were also very delightful.

"I wonder if mum misses us." Said Sky as she looked at the little butterflies floating around her.

"Oh, I hope not. She would be worried. Besides, we'll be back home in no time." Replied Joey.

While the three dogs were resting their eyes, they heard a truck coming their way. It drove up to the tree and stopped. A farmer jumped out and went on to do something in the shed nearby.

The three dogs were observing the farmer when Joey jumped and said, "Hey, guys! Look at that truck! It's heading towards the forest. Do you want to come along?"

Sky jumped with excitement and said, "Yes! Let's go; I've never been on a truck before!"

Woody hesitated for a moment but then agreed, "Okay, but let's be careful. I don't want to get into any trouble."

The three dogs ran after the truck and jumped onto the back, wagging their tails with excitement.

As the truck moved along the bumpy road, The strong wind against their fur made them feel alive as they all stood at the back with their tongues out. Looking at all the trees that passed them by, they giggled and laughed in bliss, eagerly waiting to reach the forest. After a little while on the horizon, they start seeing the forest a little.

Joey looked out and said, "Wow, the forest looks so big and beautiful from here. I can't wait to explore it!"

Sky, feeling adventurous, barked, "I want to climb the tallest tree in the forest!"

Woody, feeling nervous, whispered, "I just hope we don't run into any scary animals." After a bumpy ride, the truck finally stopped at the edge of the forest, and the dogs hopped off, feeling eager to explore.

As they all got off, ever so excited to do what they came for, they realized that there was a massive river in between them and the forest. They had to figure out a way how to cross it.

They needed to cross the river to continue their journey, but the only way across was a wobbly bridge made of old planks and ropes.

Joey said, "Okay, guys, we need to cross this bridge. But we need to be careful. It looks unstable, and we don't want to fall into the river."

Sky yelled, "I'm not scared! Let's go!"

Woody hesitated for a moment, "I don't know, guys. It looks scary."

Joey encouraged Woody, "Don't worry, Woody. We'll go across together. Just follow my lead."

The three dogs stepped onto the bridge, and it immediately started to wobble and sway. Sky charged ahead, trying to cross the bridge as quickly as possible, while Joey carefully tested each plank before putting his weight on it. Woody followed behind, trembling with fear, trying to keep up with the other two. As they reached the middle of the bridge, a gust of wind blew, and the bridge shook even more.

Sky yelped, "Whoa! This is wild!"

Joey held onto the ropes tightly, saying, "Steady now. We're almost there."

Woody closed his eyes and whispered, "I can't do this. I want to go back." But the three dogs pushed on, determined to reach the other side. They made it to the end of the bridge, panting and exhausted but proud of themselves for facing their fears and making it across the wobbly bridge as they continued on their way.

Sky said, "That was so much fun! Can we cross another wobbly bridge?"

Woody gasped and replied, "Let's just focus on the trail for now, Sky. We'll cross another bridge another day."

The dogs turned around to take a look at the fast-flowing river behind them, feeling very proud that they did that with the help of each other. At that moment, they had a small realization that if they all stick together, they might be able to achieve anything that they set their heart to.

As they got closer and closer to the forest, the smiles on their faces started to disappear, for the sight that they saw was not pretty to look at.

The forest was in shambles, and there were signs of destruction everywhere they looked.

Joey said, "What happened to the forest? It looks so different from the TV story we saw; it seems to be much worse now."

Sky curiously barked, "Let's explore and find out what's going on!"

As they walked deeper into the forest, they saw the aftermath of a wildfire that had burned through the area. Trees were charred, and the ground was blackened and lifeless. The air was still smoky, and the smell of burnt wood filled their noses.

Woody said, "It looks like there was a wildfire here recently. This is terrible. So many animals must have lost their homes."

As they walked further, they came across a river that had overflowed its banks, causing flooding and destruction. The once-clear water was now murky and brown, and the riverbank was covered in debris.

Sky looked at the flooding and said, "This is terrible! The animals that live here must be struggling to survive."

Joey felt saddened and asked, "What can we do to help?"

Woody replied, "We can't do much on our own, but now that we are here, let's take a look around and see what we can do, maybe try and get more help."

The dogs then take a moment to take it all in. With devastation all around them, they knew that they had to come up with a plan on how to take care of this situation.

"Why don't we start by going through the thick vines on our left? I think if we move in a circle and take things one by one, we can cover more ground and help more animals." Said Sky.

"That's actually not a bad idea. We should all stick together because the vines are thick, and anyone can end up getting lost." Joey replied.

And so the dogs walked further into the forest, still getting over how the smoke from the wildfires was clouding up everything around them. Making it difficult to even breathe.

"We have only been here a few minutes, and it's already so suffocating. Imagine what the animals who are trapped here feel like," said Woody

"I know. I feel so bad. That's why we're here, guys. We are going to fix this; I don't know how yet, but we will." Replied Joey with determination.

CHAPTER 4:
A FRIEND IN NEED IS A FRIEND INDEED

And so, Sky, Woody, and Joey began exploring the forest together. It was rather hot and humid. Walking in between the huge thick vines was not helping cool them down either. It was very difficult to walk while also trying to remove the vines from their faces with their paws. The dogs felt very agitated, especially Sky. She was very annoyed because of her white coat because it was now a shade of yellow and brown. Even though it annoyed her, she had a good heart and knew why she was there, to help the animals in need. And so, she pushed forward.

'I can barely see anything in here. Are you sure we're not lost?' asked Sky with an exhausted voice.

'No, I hope not. I think I can see the path now. Follow me,' said Joey as he led the group. They were walking along a trail when they heard a loud roar. Sky and Woody instantly hid behind Joey. Joey bravely stepped forward and saw a massive lion standing before them. The lion was limping and looked tired. Joey could see the sadness in the lion's eyes and knew he needed their help.

'Hello, Mr Lion,' Joey said. 'We're here to help. What seems to be the problem?'

The lion slowly came down and introduced himself as Leo. 'Thank you for offering to help me, but I don't know if you can help me. I'm afraid I'm just too big and scary.'

While the Lion seemed a little less scary now, he was still a lion, and Woody and Sky were still scared of him. His big head covered in fur was ever so magnificent. The fur around his face was blowing in the soft breeze in the forest. His paws were so huge. In fact, his entire body was so big he could eat all of them in one bite if he wanted to. But the way Leo spoke, they felt bad for him because they knew that he was in great pain. There was even a little blood.

Sky and Woody peeked out from behind Joey and said, 'Don't worry, Mr Lion. We're not scared of you. What's the matter?'

Leo sighed and explained that he and many other animals had lost their homes due to destruction. The animals had nowhere to go, and they were all very scared. Even the other lions all used to live together just beyond the vines here, we don't usually roam around these areas, but because of the flooding and the wreckage, everyone has been forced to relocate.

Joey listened carefully and then said, 'We can't let our friends suffer. We have to help them. Let's start by helping you.'

As the dogs looked at Leo, they noticed that there was a splinter in his paw. Without hesitation, they ran to his aid and helped him take out the splinter.

'Okay, this might hurt, but you will feel much better when it's out. Okay guys come on, we all need to do this together,' said Joey. Sky and Woody all got closer as Leo lifted his paw up, the splinter was huge, and it looked like it was a two-dog job. Woody and Joey volunteered. They both grabbed the end of the splinter by their teeth. In contrast, Sky had the idea that she should do a countdown so both of them pull at the same time so it doesn't hurt Leo. Everyone agreed.

'Okay, ready? 1...2...3 PULL!' she yelled.

Joey and Woody pulled as hard as they could, and in a snap, the splinter was out. Leo closed his eyes so tight and roared in pain, but it was a good kind of pain. His face lit up with joy and gratitude.

'Thank you so much!' Leo said. 'You're true friends. Will you help me find a new home? Oh, and please call me Leo. I can help you guys in return with whatever it is three little fluffballs like yourselves are doing in a place like this.'

Sky, Woody, and Joey all nodded in agreement. They thought it would be very neat to have a big scary, and powerful Lion on their side to help them out on their journey. Alas, they continued on their mission to help Leo and other animals find new homes and save the forest.

Sky, Woody, Joey and now their new friend Leo were all chatting as they walked deeper into the forest. Leo was telling them all about how the forest used to be so beautiful and green before all of the destruction took place. It was a sight to behold. The trees used to stand so tall, like a canopy. There were so many trees here that even the sunlight had trouble getting down to the ground. But the fires have destroyed everything in their path, and each day it gets worse. Leo seemed very sad while he talked about everything, but he was relieved that at least someone had come to help them. Upon walking, they realized that they were not close to a huge lake. They got closer to see what was going on when they saw a huge elephant trying to drink water from the polluted and half-dried-up lake. She looked weak and thirsty. The dogs were concerned and knew they had to help.

 Joey stepped forward and said, 'Oh, she looks so thirsty. We have to help her somehow. Come on, guys, Ideas!'

 Sky and Woody nodded in agreement. After a small discussion about what to do, they decided to dig up a small hole for the elephant and create a small stream of water from the river so that the hole they dug filled up with fresh water. The dogs got to work. Joey, Woody and Leo all took a deep breath and began digging while Sky dragged her paws in the muddy sand to lead the water to the hole.

 'Hey, this is kind of fun,' said Woody as he chuckled.

And it wasn't long before they had created a clean water source for the elephant. She drank eagerly and thanked the dogs for their help. Sky, Woody, and Joey could see that the lake was half-dried up and half-polluted due to all the debris and broken tree branches that were blocking the river. They knew they had to do something to help. Leo, the lion, joined in, and together they started removing the broken trunks and branches.

The dogs worked tirelessly, and soon the lake started filling up with fresh water. As the lake started filling up, Ellie the Elephant felt rejuvenated. She thanked the dogs and said, 'Umm, if it isn't too much trouble, I too would like to join you and save the forest.'

Sky, Woody, and Joey were thrilled to have Ellie join them. They knew that together, they could make a difference in the lives of the animals in the forest. As they set out on their journey further, Ellie led the way, using her size and strength to clear the way for the dogs. They walked for a while until they saw a group of animals huddled together, looking scared and lost. The dogs went over to see what was wrong, and they found out that the animals had lost their homes due to the destruction of the forest. They knew they had to do something to help.

Joey said, 'Let's start by building temporary new homes for them. It's all we can do for now.'

Woody added, 'And let's plant new trees to create a new habitat for them.'

'One step at a time, Woody,' replied sky as she patted him on the back.

Ellie used her strength to clear the way and help carry big leaves and wood to create a shelter to protect everyone from the pouring rain. The animals were overjoyed and thanked the dogs and Ellie for their help. As the sun began to set, the three dogs, Leo and Ellie, decided they should settle down for the night. They were tired but happy that they had made a difference in the forest on their first day as they walked around looking for a place to camp.

Joey said, 'We made a real difference today. We helped our friends in any way we could; tomorrow, we're going to do even more.'

Sky nodded in agreement, 'Yes, we did. And we made new friends too. Ellie and Leo are amazing.'

Woody smiled and said, 'We couldn't have done it without their strength and determination. They are true heroes.' And so, the dogs, Leo and now Ellie, got ready to sleep. They made their beds and lay down next to each other.

'Don't worry, guys. I'll keep the first watch. You three need some rest now,' said Leo as he volunteered to keep an eye on everyone.

As the stars came out, the forest was all quiet now. The only sound in the distance was coming from crickets. The wind brushed against the leaves and made a rustling sound. Even though it was really hot, it was very peaceful. Knowing that the three of them were together. The furballs were so tired as soon as they put their little heads down to rest, they all instantly fell asleep next to each other.

CHAPTER 5:
THE MAJESTIC UNICORN

The next morning the dogs woke up to the sound of Leo's roar. It was so loud it probably woke everyone in the forest. The sound moved through the forest like an earthquake.

'Hey, do you have to be so loud?' asked Woody as he rubbed his eyes with his little paws. Joey was just looking around, trying to make sense of what was going on. He had a funny look on his face that made Leo laugh.

'Joey, are you in there, ha-ha,' said Leo as he giggled.

Sky woke up to the sound also, but she went straight back to sleep. She didn't care what Leo or anyone had to say. She was still so tired. She didn't say it, but she missed her comfy pink doggy bed with the star pattern. It was so soft, so having to sleep on the dusty hard floor was not easy.

Ellie and Leo were chatting around, telling each other about their lives as the dogs slowly all woke up for real. Now that everyone was awake, what they needed to do now was figure out what to eat. Leo, the lion, looked around suspiciously. The dogs and everyone else was all starving.

'I'm so hungry, what do we do? I miss mum's food. I could eat the whole bag right now,' said Woody as he let out a big yawn.

'I know me too. But we have to look out for ourselves here, like the big kids. Okay, let's see, what can we eat here?' asked Joey as he paced his eyes around the forest. Looking for things that they could eat.

Ellie, the elephant, raised her trunk in the air in excitement, 'Oh oh, I know, I know a great fruit garden not far from here, we can have all the berries and coconuts we want over there...that is if it's not destroyed.'

'That sounds like a great plan. Let's go! I'm so hungry,' Sky replied while wagging her tail.

And so, the three fluffballs, Ellie the elephant and Leo the lion, all set on their way towards the garden. As everyone was walking, they were chatting about things when Leo mumbled, 'I don't really like fruits.'

'Well, I don't think we have a choice, really. It's either the fruits or we starve. I mean, it's not like you can eat us…right?' asked Joey as he looked at Leo nervously.

Leo gave him a side eye and giggled, 'Of course not…actually, never mind.'

The dogs all nervously thought that they didn't want to ask any more questions and continued on their journey in silence. Before they knew it, they had reached their destination. The garden didn't look like a garden at all. It was all in shambles. The plants were all crushed under the huge trees that fell, destroying everything on their way down. The water from the flood had washed away so much of the soil away that there was no way the fruits could have survived.

The posse looked around. Their smiles had now turned into frowns, and with their tummies grumbling, they knew they had to figure out something else. While they were all arguing about what to do next among themselves, a sudden burst of light flashed before their eyes, it blinded everyone for a few seconds. Glitter flashed from behind them, causing them to stop and turn around. As they looked in amazement, a majestic unicorn appeared before them. Her skin shimmered in the sun, and her horn glistened in the light. She was unlike anything or anyone they had ever seen before. Her skin was a shade of pink, like strawberries in yoghurt. And her eyes had all the colours of the rainbow. Everyone collectively just stood there for a moment with their jaws on the floor.

'Whoa!' exclaimed Sky, staring at the unicorn in awe. 'Is she real?'

The unicorn giggled at Sky's question and said, 'Of course, I'm real! And I'm here to help you. My name's Brittany, and I come from the clouds.'

'Help us?' asked Woody, tilting his head in confusion.

'You ask a lot of questions, okay? Here's what we'll do first. I'm sorry you guys had to come here all this way with no food but don't worry. Auntie Brittany is here to fix that,' said Brittany in an enthusiastic voice as she started hovering in midair.

The dogs, Leo and Ellie, all watched in silence as she twirled around, and a cloud of glitter formed around her. She waved her horn, and suddenly the garden behind them started to change. The garden began to flourish, with flowers blooming and trees growing tall. And then, the most amazing thing happened: the garden became full of fruit trees, with apples, pears, and plums hanging from their branches. The fairies had truly brought the garden back to life, and it was now a magical paradise full of delicious, fresh fruits.

Everyone rejoiced as they ran inside the now beautiful garden. As they entered, they saw a beautiful table set with all the different kinds of fruits they could eat, and everyone dug in. Eating like they hadn't eaten in days.

Then, Brittany, the unicorn, nodded and said, 'I've been watching you three, and I want to make things easier for you.'

The dogs looked at each other in confusion. They had no idea what the unicorn meant. Sky looked at her, still fixated on how beautiful she was.

Her mane was silky smooth in a shade of golden, sparkling in the beams coming down from the sun.

'What do you mean?' asked Joey, looking up at the unicorn.

'I mean that I have a special gift for you,' said the unicorn. 'I can grant you each a superpower that will make it easier to do what you're here to do.'

The dogs looked at each other in amazement. They had never heard of anything like this before.

'I want to be able to fly!' exclaimed Joey excitedly.

'I want to be able to run really fast,' said Sky.

'And I want to be able to duplicate myself,' said Woody.

The unicorn nodded and waved her horn around. Suddenly, a burst of energy shot out and surrounded the three dogs, granting them their powers. Joey slowly looked around towards his back, and he could see a pair of wings on his back. They were a shade of brown, just like his fur. He slowly started to flap his wings and flew up into the air.

'Woah...LOOK AT ME. I'M FLYING!' he yelled as he flew further into the air.

Joey was a bit nervous in the beginning because he was getting the hang of it, but after a few minutes of testing out his brand-new wings, he was whizzing through the forest like he was a bird.

Next came Sky. She was standing there looking at Joey while he was flying over their heads.

'Sky, my dear, why are you standing around? Why don't you try chasing your brother?' asked Brittany.

Sky looked at her with a confused face, but then she remembered what she wished for. As Joey swooshed past Sky, she started chasing him. And to her surprise, she was running as fast as he was flying, they both dodged the maze of trees in the forest like it was nothing, because of her speed she could pounce from one tree to the other and jump great distances.

'Oh my gosh, sky, you're almost as fast as me, but can you get this high up?' asked Joey as he teased Sky. She gave him the tongue as they both returned to the rest of her friends.

Woody was so excited to try out his new powers as well that he pushed and jumped, but nothing happened.

'Am I doing this right?' he asked.

'Just don't worry about it too much. Relax and focus on the beat of your heart,' replied Brittany.

Woody took a step back and closed his eyes. He grinded his teeth, trying a little too hard, one might say. But when he opened his eyes, he took a look at his brother and sister. They were all looking around him, but he managed to do it. There were now six Woodys standing before them. He was able to control each one as a separate version of himself. Instead of making them do important stuff, he made them all dance. Everyone laughed at all the funny moves he was making. While the dogs were all having fun with their newly acquired powers, The dogs were thrilled with their new powers and couldn't wait to put them to good use and help others. As they played, Brittany the unicorn watched them, amused by their antics. Brittany interrupted them.

'Listen, boys and girls, now that you have your powers. You have to promise me that you will only use them to help others and to do good in the world. I am trusting you with this.'

'We promise!' the three dogs replied in harmony.

'Well, my work here is done. I will leave you to it then. See you all later, toodles,' she replied as she disappeared into a pink cloud right before everyone's eyes.

And so, the dogs, Ellie and Leo, all resumed their journey to save the forest.

CHAPTER 6: ANIMALS IN DISTRESS

Everyone was walking around the forest. It was a rather tiring day. The dogs, with their newfound powers, had been helping twice as many animals in need. Everyone was exhausted from the heat, and they just wanted a small escape to a cool stream nearby. As they were all walking around looking for what to do, Woody heard something.

'Wait, what is that...I think I hear something,' he said as he twisted his ears back and forth.

'I don't hear anything, Woody. Are you sure you're not losing your marbles? All I hear is the forest,' said Sky with a sarcastic tone.

There was a faint sound in the air that only Woody was able to hear, but it wasn't loud enough to make out where it was coming from. Woody had a bright idea to get higher, he duplicated himself, and they all grabbed on a leaning tree nearby. One by one, the duplicates climbed on top of each other, and Woody came last. He was high enough to try and see what that sound was. He could hear much better now—it appeared as if someone was in trouble.

'I hear sounds of distress, guys. I think there are some babies in trouble. I don't know how I know this, but you have to trust me. I hear them, and they need our help,' said Woody.

'Oh dear...what's going on?' asked Ellie in a concerned voice.

'If what Woody said is true, then we must check it out. Someone might actually need our help,' replied Leo.

Sky and Joey both agreed, and they all started following Woody. He led them through a lot of scary places, but they all trusted him and followed his lead. The sounds were getting louder and louder as they were getting closer. He led them through a very dark cave where they could hear bats.

'I'm really scared. Can someone stay close to me? I can barely see anything, and I'm really scared of bats," said Sky as she was drenched with fear. Joey came closer to her and walked with her. When they crossed the cave, they were now faced with a giant hill. It had a bumpy climb. Joey flew over it like it was nothing, but the rest of them had to be careful with where they stepped because it was slippery.

When they were on the tippy top of the hill, Joey asked Woody if they were close.

'Hey, buddy! Are we there yet?' He asked as he fluttered his wings in the air.

'I uh…I don't know. I could hear them, but now all I can hear is the stupid river,' he replied with an annoyed look as he tried to focus on where the sound was coming from.

Everyone looked at him, waiting for him to figure out what it was that he heard, slowly growing impatient, wondering whether there even was a sound in the beginning.

'Oh wait, I hear it again. I think it's coming from the East. Hey Joey, can you fly up and see if you see any birds in need of help?' asked Woody.

'On it,' Joey replied.

And so, Joey went up into the air and started to look around. After a few minutes of searching in between the thick trees, he spotted a couple of yellow birds who were on top of a tree that looked like it was about to break. The tree was in the way of the extremely fast-flowing river, and they needed to be helped as soon as possible because the babies in the nest looked like they couldn't fly.

'I see them. They're over here,' said Joey as everyone followed the sound of his voice.

Joey flew closer to the birds and offered to help. He slowly and gently flew closer to the nest and set his paws down on one of the branches. He peeked inside the nest, and there were four little baby birds who were all crying. Their parents were both by their sides, trying to figure out how to get them to safety before the tree broke down.

'I'm here to help. Put your babies on my back, and I can get them to safety...hurry! The water's getting stronger. I don't think it will hold much longer," he yelled over the sound of the gushing water.

The parents quickly placed their babies on Joey's back one by one, and he flew them down safely to the ground.

'Oh, thank you so much. You saved us all. How can we ever repay you?' asked mama bird as she wiped her tear. She was so happy to see all her babies safe and sound.

'No need, ma'am. That's what we're here to do. You can thank this guy right here. He's the one who found you," said Joey as he pulled Woody towards him.

Woody nodded in excitement, excited to see that he actually helped save some lives. The parrots thanked him as they tended to their babies. The rest of the gang all clapped for Woody.

'Aww...you guys don't have to do that. I am just happy that I could be of help. I guess Brittany didn't tell me I have stronger senses now, too," he said.

As the day went on, everybody decided they had earned a little break, and so they all settled down next to a cool stream nearby. The sound of the water rushing downhill was very soothing to the ears. Ellie and Sky were chatting away like little girls while the boys splashed around in the water, trying to get each other wet.

They were enjoying the peaceful scenery and the cool breeze that tickled their fur. They found a nice spot under a tree and decided to rest for a while. They lay down on the grass and enjoyed the warmth of the sun. Suddenly, they heard some loud noises coming from the nearby bushes. Joey jumped up and barked, ready to protect his friends. Sky and Woody looked at him, confused.

'What's wrong, Joey?' Woody asked.

'I heard something in the bushes,' Joey replied. His ears perked up. They all got up and cautiously approached the bushes. As they peeked through the leaves, they saw a zebra and a parrot arguing with each other. They were at each other's throats, and the dogs felt like they needed to butt in before somebody got hurt, even though it was funny how a zebra and parrot were in an argument together,

'What are they arguing about?' Sky asked.

'I don't know,' Joey replied.

'Let's find out...' Joey walked towards the arguing animals and barked loudly. The zebra and the parrot froze in surprise and stared at Joey.

'What's going on here?' Joey asked.

The zebra and the parrot looked at each other and then back at Joey.

'Who are you?' the parrot asked.

'I'm Joey, and these are my friends Sky, Woody, Ellie, and Leo,' Joey replied. 'We were passing through and wanted to check out the noise. We heard you arguing and wanted to know what's going on.'

The zebra and the parrot looked at each other and then back at Joey.

'Well,' the zebra said. 'We're arguing about who should find a new home first.'

'Our homes were destroyed,' the parrot added.

'We need to find new ones as soon as possible,' Joey and everyone else looked at each other, understanding the situation.

'Don't worry,' Joey said. 'We'll help you find new homes in no time. Why don't you come with us?'

The zebra and the parrot looked at each other and then back at Joey.

'Really?' the parrot asked.

'Of course,' Sky replied.

'We're all friends here. Let's go!' she said.

The zebra and the parrot introduced themselves as they smiled and followed the dogs and their friends.

'I'm Zoe. I used to live nearby, and this is Palo. He talks a lot, and when I say a lot, I mean he doesn't know when to stop talking,' she said while looking at Palo and giggling.

'Yeah? And what about you? You're so annoying I could fly away every time you open your mouth.' replied Palo with a smirk.

'But regardless, we have been best friends for a long time, and I can't imagine a day without this bird,' said Zoe, and upon hearing that, Palo smiled.

They walked together through the woods, searching for new homes. They chatted and laughed, and the zebra and the parrot told Joey and his friends about their adventures. After a while, they found a beautiful meadow with a pond and some trees.

'This is a perfect place for you, Zoe,' Joey said to the zebra.

'And you, Palo, can live in that tree over there,' Sky said, pointing at a tall tree. The zebra and the parrot looked at their new homes, feeling happy and grateful.

'I mean, they can work for the time being, considering the state our forest is in. Thank you so much,' Zoe said as she hugged Joey.

'We couldn't have done it without you,' Palo added as he, too, hugged Sky and Woody.

The dogs asked if they wanted to come along. They could use an extra pair of hands. They told them all about how they helped Ellie and Leo out, and now they're all travelling together trying to help other animals in need. Both Zoe and Palo agreed in a heartbeat.

'That sounds like fun. Count us in!'

They both said, and so, the now-grown group of friends all walked together, resuming their journey.

CHAPTER 7: THE POOR LAMB

The dogs and the rest of the gang were busy exploring new parts of the forest and discovering new things. Soon enough, they decided to explore a part of the forest they had never been to before. Joey pointed south, and Palo the Parrot gasped.

'What's wrong?' Joey asked.

'You don't want to go there. It's a scary place. I've seen many animals get stuck there. Right up ahead, you will see a huge ditch, it's really deep, and I've heard if someone ever falls in, they don't ever come out,' he replied as he flapped his wings and sat on Zoe's back.

'Oh, but we have to go that way. There's nowhere else to go. Why don't we take a look and see how it goes? We'll be careful,' said Joey as he started to walk, and so everyone followed him nervously.

Ellie and Leo knew what Palo was talking about. They had seen it before but only from afar. They were telling dog stories every once in a while, and they would often hear about animals getting lost in the pit. Sky was a little scared.

'I don't know about this, guys. Maybe we should turn back...I'm sure there's another way,' she said with her tail tucked between her legs.

As they were walking, following Joey's lead, they came across a dangerous pit. It was deep and dark, and anyone could fall inside. They knew they had to be careful. The pit looked like it was never-ending, and it got darker on the way down.

Woody had the bright idea to toss a rock in to see how deep it was. He picked up a rock in his mouth and tossed it in. As the rock fell in, everybody watched curiously, waiting to hear the sound of it hitting the ground, but there was none. Then, Leo pushed in a bigger rock, but still the same thing. There was no sound of the rocks hitting the ground.

'Okay, so we know that it's extremely deep, and we have to be careful, but what we can do is we all hold each other's paws, legs or even tails. Just grab on to the person next to you, and we can cross it in no time,' said Joey.

The path was very small and dangerous, but they could do it if they all stuck together. Ellie was in a bit of a pickle because she was the biggest animal out of all of them, and she had to be extra careful. She volunteered to go in last. The gang agreed and held hands as they walked around the pit.

'Okay, here we go...nice and easy. Everyone, keep your eyes on the path and don't make any sudden movements. Take it easy! Just follow me,' said Joey as he took the lead. He carefully looked where he stepped, making sure his friends were safe as well.

'Okay, you guys are almost there. I can see the end. Just a few more minutes of walking,' said Palo as he flew above them, looking at the path they were following and helping them out.

'Open your eyes, Sky. I'm here, but you can't just walk with your eyes closed; it's too dangerous!' he pointed out as he gave a little nudge.

Leo, Ellie and Zoe were in the back, while Sky, Woody, and Joey were in the front. They were all making great progress with the help of teamwork when suddenly Joey slipped.

'We're doing so goo- AAAA!' yelled Joey as he tumbled down. Woody bent down to grab him, but he fell. He couldn't get a grip.

'JOEY!' yelled Sky.

Joey very quickly disappeared into the dark; nobody could see him anymore. Everyone just stood there in shock. Just standing there with horrified looks on their faces, everyone didn't know what to do when Sky started crying.

'Joey, come back,' she whispered as tears were streaming down her face. Woody just froze, looking down towards the dark pit as he was frozen. He didn't know what to do either. Then, a voice surprised them from behind, and they all turned around in a hurry to see if what they thought was real.

'Hey guys, why the long faces?' Joey asked as he fluttered around in the air above them.

'I forgot that I can fly!' Joey recalled.

He flapped his wings and easily flew back up to the top of the pit and joined the rest of the gang. Everyone was amazed and relieved that Joey was safe.

'That was close,' Woody said. 'I'm glad you remembered you could fly.'

'Yeah, me too,' Joey replied.

After that close call, the dogs and the rest of their friends quickly crossed the pit. Now that everyone was safe and sounded on the other side, they resumed their journey into the unknown. But then, Woody started sniffing around. He climbed on top of a rock and started moving his nose around in the air. He had an increased sense of smell and could sense that someone was in danger. He followed his nose, and the other dogs followed him. He led them towards the edge of the cliff, back to the pit. As the three of them looked down, they saw a baby lamb stuck on one of the ledges. It appeared that he had slipped and fallen. He was crying and felt so helpless. The dogs all felt so bad for him and knew that they needed to help the lamb immediately.

'Oh no, we have to help her,' Sky insisted.

The gang quickly figured out their options on how to help her. They worked together and managed to get her out of the pit. Ellie came in and suggested something. 'I have an idea! I could lower my trunk down to the lamb and maybe try to scoop her up if I can reach her,' she said.

While the rest of the party was busy figuring out what to do, Joey flew down to the lamb to comfort her and help her. He slowly fluttered down and told the lamb that there was nothing to worry about.

'Hey, little one! It's okay. We're here to help. My friends are figuring out what to do as we speak,' said Joey in a reassuring voice.

'Hello, I'm scared, and I just want to go home,' Sweetie replied as she tried to hide her face. She had been stuck there for almost an hour, and she was trembling.

'Don't worry, Sweetie. We'll help you find your home,' Joey reassured.

'Hey Joey, you there?' yelled Woody.

'Yeah, I'm here. What's up? Do you guys have a plan?' asked Joey.

'Yeah!' replied Woody.

Joey flew back up to the rest of his friends after telling Sweetie that he'll be back in no time.

'Okay...so here's the plan. I will slide down to Sweetie and use my duplicates to give her some height. She can climb on my back, and I'll lift her up as high as I can and then Ellie will be able to grab her by her trunk and scoop her up,' explained Woody.

'That sounds like a great plan,' Joey replied.

Everyone hurried by the cliffside and got to work. Woody slowly slid his decoys down to Sweetie, one by one, and told her not to worry. Sweetie then climbed on top one by one, and then Ellie lowered her trunk. Ever so gently, she wrapped it around Sweetie and slowly pulled her up.

'Hurray! That was amazing,' said Sky as she wagged her tail in the air while Leo, Palo, and Zoe all rejoiced and introduced themselves to Sweetie.

'Hi, my name is Sweetie. My parents and I were going somewhere when there a storm hit us, and I lost them. I don't know where they are, and I just want to see them again. Will you help me?' asked Sweetie the lamb with tears in her eyes.

'Of course, we will. You don't have to worry about anything,' said Woody as he patted her on the back. Suddenly, they were interrupted by a wildfire in the distance that erupted spontaneously. They all got a little scared and decided to take Sweetie with them and help her to find her parents later. The crew was now bigger than ever.

'Hey guys, let's just take a moment to look around. I'm so thankful to have all of you by my side. I didn't imagine that I would make so many friends. First Leo, then Ellie, then came to the chatty duo Zoe and Palo. And now our smallest friend Sweetie. You all are amazing. I just wanted to put that out there,' said Joey

'Oh, come on, man. You're going to make us all teary,' said Palo, and everyone laughed.

And so, Sweetie, now by their side, they all went back to their journey to save the forest. Even though they had helped so many people along the way, there was still so much to do, and so many animals left to save.

CHAPTER 8: OVERCOMING ONE HURDLE AFTER ANOTHER

The forest was now in desperate need of a makeover. After helping so many animals on the way, the gang now decided to take care of things on a bigger scale. They thought that they needed to give the forest an uplift because everything was a mess. Smoke in the distance from the wildfires that were erupting periodically. Wiping large areas of plant life in its way, forcing animals to evacuate. The floods that were causing the forest grounds to be inhabitable. The broken trees and branches scattered everywhere, blocking paths for animals to get to safety. It was a lot of work, and so the dogs and their friends all decided on a plan to split up.

'I will take Ellie and Zoe with me. We, girls, need to stick together. Also, I think I can control the weather. Yesterday, while you were all busy, I think I made it rain, but I might be wrong. Anyway, we can take the east end and get started over there. What do you say, Ellie and Zoe?' she asked as she walked over to them with a smile on her face.

'Sounds like a plan. Girls to the rescue!' said Ellie as she and Zoe both got excited to get started.

"I can help by clearing the paths for the animals to return home. I can duplicate myself and cover more ground. My decoys can help me with added strength to help clear out the bigger trees. I can take, um...why don't I take Palo with me? He can help me spot things from the air. I think together we can be a good team,' said Woody.

'Let's do it! I will be your eyes in the Sky. You can count on me!' replied Palo as he flew around in the air.

'And I can fly around the canopy to spot any animals in distress that can't be seen otherwise and help them out of danger,' added Joey, who had the help of his trusty new wings.

The three siblings knew they had to act fast to save the forest and all the animals living in it. Sky used her powers to change the weather and make it rain. The rain helped to stop the wildfire and water the lakes in the forest. Sky could even contain the water, she spun her tail around, and the overflowing water simply lifted up in the air in a spiral and turned into vapour, making everything around them much cooler and nicer.

'Wow! Thanks, Sky! Your rain has saved us,' said a family of rabbits who had been stuck in the forest.

Woody used his decoys. He created ten this time, showing that he had much more control over his abilities now. He used them to clear the paths for the animals to return home. He helped a group of deer, who were lost in the forest, find their way back to their families.

'Thank you, Woody! We couldn't have made it without your help!' said the deer, grateful for his assistance.

Joey flew around the canopy, looking for animals in distress. He spotted so many birds that needed help, and he then, one by one, helped everyone who was trapped in a tree that had caught fire or that was about to fall apart.

'Quick! Follow me!' said Joey as he flew down to the tree.

The birds followed Joey's lead and flew away to safety. Joey's keen eyesight had helped him spot the birds in danger, and his wings had allowed him to reach them quickly. He was so grateful to Brittany for how she gave him this power. He couldn't have done half as much without them.

'Thank you, Joey! We are so grateful for your help!' said the birds, relieved to have been rescued.

While Joey, Sky and Woody were busy doing bigger things by using their superpowers, the other animals felt that they should be doing more. So, while the dogs were running around left and right, Leo, Ellie, Zoe, and Palo were doing their own thing.

'We need to do something about this. Let's all help as much as we can in our own ways,' said Leo.

Ellie used her big, strong trunk to lift heavy logs and clear paths for the animals. Zoe used her sharp eyesight to spot any animals in trouble, and she helped them out of danger. Palo flew around the forest, delivering messages and keeping everyone informed. As they were working, they heard a loud sneeze. It was Sweetie who had accidentally blown away a lot of dirt and messy tree branches out of the way with her super breath.

'What just happened?" asked Sweetie, surprised at what she had done.

'It looks like you have superpowers, Sweetie,' said Sky, amazed at her ability. 'You can use your super breath to help animals too!'

Sweetie was thrilled to learn that she had superpowers and started helping out immediately. She used her super breath to blow away dirt and leaves, making it easier for animals to move around. At the same time, everyone was busy helping around.

Meanwhile, Joey was flying around when he spotted two lambs looking around. They seemed stressed, so Joey approached them and asked them what was going on.

'Oh, we're looking for our baby. We lost her along the way, and now we can't find her. Can you help us?' asked the mama lamb.

'Ha-ha, you are Sweetie's parents. You have nothing to worry about. Follow me!' he said as he excitedly led them back to the group. When the parents saw their little baby safe, they were very grateful to Joey for reuniting them.

'MUM! DAD!' yelled Sweetie as soon as she saw her parents.

'Thank you so much, Joey! We were so worried about Sweetie!' said Sweetie's parents, relieved to have their baby back.

As they continued to work, the forest began to look better. The birds started making new homes in the trees, and the river began flowing again, making the water cleaner so that animals that lived in the water could thrive. Everything was falling into place, and it was all because of all the hard work the animals put in, with the help of teamwork.

'This is amazing!' said Leo, looking around at the beautiful forest they had helped restore. 'We make a great team!'

'Indeed, we do,' agreed Ellie, smiling.

As they were admiring their work, they heard a loud howl. It was the pack of wolves that lived in the forest, and they were in trouble. The wolves have not been nice to the rest of the animals in the forest, and everyone hates them. They would bully and scare the smaller animals away. But this time, they were in a pickle. A big tree had fallen, blocking their path and separating them from their den.

'We have to help them,' said Zoe, determined to lend a hand.

'Should we? Remember when they came and scared you away, Zoe,' said Palo with a sad face.

'They may be bad, but they're asking for our help, and we can't just let them be. We have to do something. Maybe they'll change if we show them kindness,' said Joey as he rounded everyone up to help out.

They all worked together to lift the tree and clear the path for the wolves. Once they had done so, the wolves ran to their den, grateful for the help.

'Thank you for saving us,' said the leader of the pack. 'We owe you our lives and an apology for how bad we have been in the past. You have my word that we will change. Thank you for all the work you have been doing.'

'We were happy to help,' said Joey, smiling.

As they were walking back to their homes, they saw that the sun was setting. It had been a long day, but they had accomplished so much.

'I had a great time today,' said Sweetie, smiling.

'Me too," said Palo, nodding his head.

'Same here,' said Zoe, grinning.

'I'm glad we could all work together and help the animals in the forest,' said Ellie, looking around at her friends.

'Me too,' said Leo, smiling. 'And I have a feeling that there will be many more adventures to come.'

Together, the three dogs and their friends saved the forest and all the animals living in it. The other animals in the forest also helped out in their own way, and they all celebrated their victory with a big feast.

'We did it! We saved the forest!' shouted Sky, Woody, and Joey, happy and proud of their accomplishment.

'Yay! Let's all celebrate and have some fun!' said the other animals as they danced and sang together.

From that day on, the forest was a happy and safe place for all its inhabitants. The three dogs continued to play and explore the forest, always ready to help when needed. And all the animals knew that they could count on their three brave friends to keep them safe and sound.

CHAPTER 9: BEST FRIENDS FOREVER

After playing around for hours with everyone, it was time, even though it was going to be hard. They knew they had to go. Sky, Joey, and Woody were very happy with how they were able to do so much for all the animals in the forest. They looked around and smiled at each other, knowing that they had made a difference. But as the trio exited the forest, they realized that their powers had vanished.

They looked at each other, a little sad and confused. Suddenly, Brittany showed up out of nowhere.

'Hey guys,' she said as she shimmered in the sun. 'Why the long faces?'

'Our powers are gone,' said Joey, with a sad look on his face. 'We don't know what to do.'

Brittany looked at them and smiled. She said, 'Oh, don't worry, guys. Your powers can only work inside the forest because it's a magical forest. And you were given your powers to help others. If you return to the forest, your powers will be back.'

Sky, Joey, and Woody looked at each other, feeling hopeful.

'Really?' they asked.

'Yes, really,' replied Brittany. 'Trust me, I know.'

'And if you hurry back to the forest, you'll be just in time for our annual get-together. I'm a new friend to you, but I often visit the forest. We do a party every year, and we would love it if you could join us this year,' said Brittany excited to spend more time with the dogs.

Brittany told them how proud she was of all of them. The three siblings were the bravest dogs she had ever met.

'I can't thank you enough for all that you have done for everyone, I wish I could let you keep your powers outside the forest, too, but I don't have control over that. You see, even my powers come from the forest,' she explained to the dogs.

Sky, Joey, Woody, and Brittany looked at each other and smiled, knowing that they had made a lifelong friend.

'We're so happy we met you,' said Sky, feeling proud to have made such a caring friend.

'We sure did,' replied Joey, with a smile on his face.

'Thanks for your help, Brittany,' said Woody, wagging his tail. 'We couldn't have done it without you.'

Brittany smiled. 'Anytime, guys. That's what friends are for. But I'm afraid all good things must come to an end. It's time for me to go tend to my duties elsewhere. I will miss you, but here take this. It's a special stone,' she said as she handed all three of them a pink rock. It magically attached itself to each other of their collars. The stone was a shiny hue of pink and orange, and it was glowing slightly.

'It will help you find me whenever you need my help with anything in the world, just brush on the stone once, and I will come to you in a jiffy,' said Brittany with a smile on her face.

'Oh, wow, that's so cool. Thank you so much,' replied Sky with excitement in her voice. As Brittany said goodbye, a pink foggy cloud started to form around her, and she vanished just like that.

It had been a long and tiring day for Sky, Joey, and Woody. They had spent most of their day hanging out with their friends in the forest, making sure that all the animals were safe and sound.

Leo, Ellie, Zoe, and Palo were all with them with sad faces because they knew that their furry friends had to leave.

'Will you come back soon?' asked Leo as he shed a tear.

'Oh, Leo...look at you. That face doesn't look good on you. You're supposed to be the strong one among all of us,' replied Joey as he wiped the tear off Leo's cheek.

'It was very nice knowing you three. We will miss you too,' said both Zoe and Palo.

'We'll miss you both too. Try to keep out of trouble, and oh, I almost forgot. Try not to fight with each other,' said Sky as she chuckled.

Ellie, the elephant, was rather quiet. She was standing a little farther away from everyone with a sad face observing everyone. The dogs looked at her and noticed that she was sad, and so they went over to check up on her.

'Hey, Ellie, what's up? Why are you standing all the way here?' asked Joey.

'I don't know how to say this, but I've never made many friends in my life. I'm very shy and because I'm so big everyone gets scared of me. Even if I try to be nice to them, so, after you guys came, I have had the time of my life, and now after you're gone, I will miss you,' she told the dogs while staring at the ground.

'Oh silly! You have so many new friends now who love you and want to be friends with you for who you are, not what you look like,' said Sky as she rubbed her fur against Ellie's leg, trying to comfort her.

Leo, Zoe, and Palo overheard this conversation, and they came running. They all huddled around Ellie and gave her a big hug. Her heart was now full of warm fuzzy feelings seeing that she indeed had friends.

'Don't be silly. You have us now. We're your friends,' said Zoe.

'Best friends!' added Palo.

The sun was starting to set, and the dogs knew it was time to say goodbye. They said farewell to all their friends with teary eyes as they set on their journey back home. All the animals in the forest waved at them as they were leaving. The dogs were sad but happy at the same time; it was all very bittersweet.

After reaching home, they were worried that mum was going to be mad at them for disappearing like that for so many days. They quietly crept up the driveway and into the living room through their doggy door, gently walking around looking for mum.

'Where is she? Oh boy, she's going to be so mad. I'm scared,' said Sky as she hid behind the sofa.

Suddenly they heard footsteps approaching from the kitchen. It was mum.

'Oh, there you are. I have been looking for you three for five minutes now. It's time for your dinner. Come along,' she demanded.

The dogs all looked at each other, completely confused as to what had happened.

'Uh, what was that? Did she just say five minutes?' asked Woody as he tilted his head. As they were arguing about what was going on. Suddenly the stones on their collars twinkled altogether. And they knew.

'BRITTANNY!' they all yelled.

It was a sign from Brittany that she had something to do with this. Time back home had slowed down so that mum wouldn't worry too much about her babies missing. And so, the dogs all gobbled up their dinner; they missed mum's food so much. After that, they decided it was time to rest and went to the living room and settled down on the carpet right in front of the TV.

'I wonder how our friends in the forest are doing?' asked Sky with a sigh.

'I hope they're all doing well. I'm sure they are,' replied Joey. 'But I do miss them. It's not the same without them around.'

'I know what you mean,' said Woody with a yawn. 'But we did a good job. We helped a lot of animals in need.'

'Yeah, we make a pretty good team,' said Joey, with a laugh.

The three dogs looked at each other and smiled. They knew that they had made a difference for a lot of animals that needed their help. They started remembering all the different things they did, like helping the birds and her babies to safety. Help Sweetie reunite with her parents. Even the wolves, they helped them too. It was an adventure of a lifetime. They laughed and smiled, knowing that they had helped those in need. They were grateful for their powers and for each other.

'We make a great team,' said Woody, with a smile on his face.

'We sure do,' replied Sky, with a nod.

'And I wouldn't want to go on an adventure with anyone else,' added Joey.

The three dogs looked at each other and smiled. They knew that they were a special team, and they couldn't wait to see what adventures awaited them in the future. Suddenly They were interrupted by a piece of breaking news on the telly.

'There have been many reports that the ocean is in grave danger, the marine life is at great risk and needs immediate attention. A lot of fish are barely surviving because of the polluted waters,' reported the reporter on the screen.

The dogs all looked at each other with that same look they had when they decided to go to the forest and smiled. Knowing exactly what their next adventure was going to be.

About the Author

Lauren Meehan is the owner and founder of *Catch It* in *Moment Photography Studios* based in King's Langley. She has always loved animals from a very young age and she grew up with dogs and horses. Currently, Lauren has 3 beautiful dogs named Woody, Joey, and Sky Witch. Her recent publication titled, *The Adventures of Benmore Dogs,* revolves around her dogs for the readers to meet.